Finding Your Perfect Sexual Match:
A Man and Woman's Quick Reference
Guide to Love, Marriage and Intimacy
Using Astrology

Copyright © 2016 by Lysa London

ISBN 978-0-9785056-6-0

All rights reserved. No part of this book may be reproduced, scanned or distributed in any manner whatsoever without the prior written permission of the author except in the case of brief quotation embodied in critical articles and reviews.

Finding Your Perfect Match:
Man and Woman's Quick Reference Guide to
Love, Marriage and Intimacy Using Astrology

By Lysa London

Finding Your Perfect Sexual Match by Lysa London

This book is about sex. You need romance, but when the romance is over, you'd better be left with good sex. There's a difference between how you want to be handled in the bedroom-compared to the rest of the house. You deserve sexual compatibility and fulfillment.

That said, this book is straight forward, steamy and spot on. As a rule of thumb, **to keep your man sexually satisfied you must be a lady in the streets and a freak in the sheets**. Men, you must adhere to the very same standards.

The stars and planets –moon and stars create alignments that can lead you to your perfect sexual match. The science of sex will always lead back to astrology. Sex is a mind- body experience. In this book, you will find out how to connect both- at the same time.

Finding Your Perfect Sexual Match by Lysa London

This is not some long, bland zodiac reading. This title provides quick, direct and exclusive insight into the sexual mind of your love interest.
This title lists specifically what a man or woman needs to know in order to keep their partner sexually fulfilled. It also takes the guesswork out of dating and sexual compatibility.

It's not enough to seduce a lover if you can't hold on to them afterwards. You must stimulate their secret nature in the bedroom or the next person will.

You can find love, sex and happiness if you study the compatibility of your love interest. The fulfillment of your needs as well as your mates is the foundation of every relationship-especially sexual. Learn emotional and sexual secrets that will keep you ahead of the game.

Lysa London

Finding Your Perfect Sexual Match by Lysa London

Section 1: For Women

Signs/Contents

Aquarius..... 5

Pisces......... 9

Aries........... 13

Taurus........ 16

Gemini........ 20

Cancer......... 24

Leo.............. 29

Virgo............ 34

Libra............ 39

Scorpio........ 44

Sagittarius... 49

Capricorn..... 53

Section 2: For Men...57

The Aquarius Man

Aquarius is the water bearer
(January 20-February 18)

Women: To reach the Aquarius male you have to start with his mind. You must first stimulate his intellectual juices; otherwise you will not fulfill him sexually. Aquarius is a people person. He's generous and interested in helping others solve their problems. He will analyze the problem and search for an answer. If you want to catch his eye and get his attention, pretend like you've got a problem; he's anxious to help. This smart, creative man is easy to get next to-don't be timid.

Aquarius men are shy, so you'll have to make the first move. If you land a date with him, kindly suggest where you'd like to go. No matter how enticed or excited you are, become his friend before offering him anything else. The **Aquarius** male doesn't like to work hard, doesn't like to explain himself and doesn't like an overbearing woman. He'll try to play it cool but he's very emotional.

He doesn't like to follow rules or restrictions. Don't back him into a corner. He likes to fly free; independence and travel. He has friends but no deep ties. He likes to meet people but can become bored with them. In sports and business he loves a challenge. He's always on the go so don't expect him to sit around the house.

In a relationship he can be soft and gentle. But he can be sidetracked by self gratification. He wants the perfect mate but is not so quick to get married. It will take a long time before he pops the question. He's kind and able to read people.

The Aquarius man is friendly and likable. His personable attitude is what draws people to him. So don't be jealous. He can sometimes have weird, eclectic tastes but he flirts more out of curiosity then lust; so don't panic and smother him.

Finding Your Perfect Sexual Match by Lysa London

How to Sex the Aquarius Man

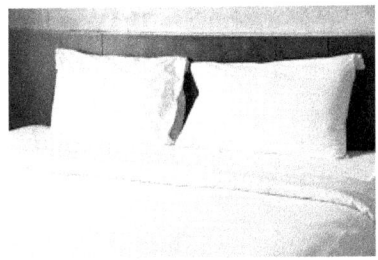

The **Aquarius** man likes a woman for what's inside – not just outside. He likes to enjoy foreplay before digging in; it's pretty much mandatory. He likes to give women oral sex. He really gets into it. So, you may orgasm before he even penetrates you.

And he doesn't mind using toys, lubricants, whatever; just ask. He likes new positions, sensations and erotica. He may also try swapping. His tastes may often fall on the perverse side. And don't look for any remorse when he gets caught either.

He's the most open minded of all the signs- and is always sexually curious. Don't let him get bored. Try different positions. Some **Aquarius** males can tend to be bi-sexual. They like to experiment, so keep your eyes open. He likes toys and devices.

He can be easily led into sadism or sadomasochism; whips, chains and spikes. He's open to threesomes, too. Remember, **Aquarius** is a private person. So keep your freak, nasty business to yourself.

The **Aquarius** man likes church. And that's where the biggest freaks are found. He loves music too; so concerts, parties, clubs and gatherings are his hangouts. You can use your ipod or mixed c.d. to spark up a conversation. Talk about pollution, politics or social issues and you've got his undivided attention.

You can spot an **Aquarius** man from across a crowded room; he's the one having the interesting conversation. He likes an assertive woman, so don't be afraid to make the first move. Don't be boring and avoid run-in-the-mill dates. Now, go out there and catch yourself an **Aquarius** man!

The Aquarius Male is most compatible with Libra, Sagittarius and Aquarius Women.

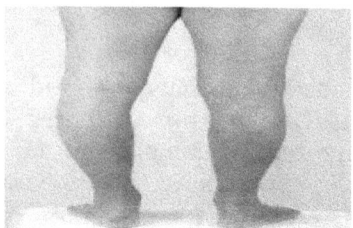

Rub warm oil on the back of his legs and watch how excited he becomes.

Finding Your Perfect Sexual Match by Lysa London

The Pisces Man

Pisces is the Symbol of the Two Fish (Feb 19th—Mar 20th)

Ladies, the **Pisces** man is unpredictable. You just don't know what he's going to do next. He will often say one thing and do another, but you just don't know. He's sensitive and receptive and genuinely tries to see the good in people. He's attracted to sexy, provocative women who are bossy and in control.

He can be considered a bit gullible and often lured into a fantasy land. His woman and life must be a storybook romance. He is a private person who believes that what happens in the bedroom stays in the bedroom. He'll have a hard time being faithful because certain women can easily push his buttons.

He often lives for and in the moment; so you'll have to really be a strong willed, loving influence to keep him on the right path. Think of yourself as a rock that's always there and consistent; in order to stay your Pisces man.

At the club **Pisces** man is quite charismatic and watched by everyone. His pleasant demeanor makes him approachable by many. He keeps the mood festive. Ask him out to poetry night or to an art show.

Appeal to his artistic nature. Talk about extraterrestrials or haunted houses. They like the unusual. Notice his suit, hat or shoes and tell him how good they look.

Pisces love to drink. Find out his limit before he starts shoveling drinks down his throat. The term *'drinks like a fish,'* refers to the **Pisces**. They need a strong woman and partner; borderline bully to keep him from running wild.

He's not one to settle down. And if he does say I do, he's got his eye on one of your bridesmaids while he's saying it. He likes to eat high off the hog, spoiling himself and you. So much so that he forgets about the bills have to be paid tomorrow.

It's best that your **Pisces** man hang around with positive people. Negative people's bad habits tend to rub off on him. He's creative and talented with his hands; an ideas man, who doesn't care for blue collar work. He can be a bit of a shirker so don't expect him to get his hands dirty.

He isn't good at listening or dolling out advice, but is easily seduced by people who live wild lives-and often being a follower, his lack of self esteem will cause him to indulge in whatever illegal or toxic activities they are into. He's warm and sensitive to those in his zone so don't be too hard on him.

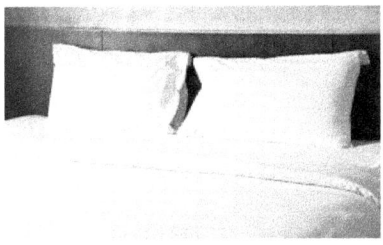

How to Sex the Pisces Man

The **Pisces** man wants it when he wants it; no excuses or delays. If you don't, the next woman will; single, married or divorced. It doesn't matter. He'll do them all. But he prefers older women who know what the hell they're doing in the bedroom. He follows the sexual lead of the woman he's with. Whatever sexual fetish she desires he will oblige.

Pisces man has a foot fetish. He loves to touch, rub and suck women's toes. So if you're planning on sexing a **Pisces** man you'd better have well groomed and manicured feet. If you like it rough he'll oblige you. If you prefer to tie him up and spank him, he's also game. He enjoys it when you get on top and ride then let him cum in your mouth.

Whatever the woman wants **Pisces** wants- too. From freaky fetishes to role play and spankings, he's down. He's one of a few signs that will play dress up if you ask him to; very uninhibited. **Pisces** man also has an addictive sexual persona. He loves anything that gets him off spectacularly. But remember, pain and pleasure are his forte. He likes to feel pain with his pleasure. It heightens his orgasm. Examples: squeezing the testicles or biting his nipples.

If you're too scared to suck his toes-
then wash and massage his feet.
 It drives Pisces crazy.

Finding Your Perfect Sexual Match by Lysa London

The Aries Man

Aries is the Symbol of the Ram
(March 21-April19)

Ladies, it may seem like the **Aries** man consumes a lot of energy drinks but he doesn't. He's naturally hyper. He likes to shake things up; a real live action hero. Sometimes he's a tight wad, other times he'll spend every dime in his pocket. He's a rule beaker and natural born heartbreaker.

The **Aries** man is down for sex whenever and wherever- so be ready. An ex- boyfriend will not be tolerated calling you or hanging around. In fact, male friends are barely tolerated because **Aries** has a huge jealous streak. He's passionate, wild and unpredictable when it comes to sex. He goes for the gusto-making sure you're satisfied. But a pure **Aries** is Sadistic; he gets pleasure from your pain.

Finding Your Perfect Sexual Match by Lysa London

You've got to keep it 100 as they say, to catch the attention of an **Aries** man. They're good, sympathetic listeners, but don't talk them to death about nonsense and don't play games; it's a definite turn off. Remember, he's a thrill seeker so keep him excited. **Aries** men like extreme sports. And in quiet times a good book with serious plots.

He has an ego and can be self indulged so give him realistic compliments. Although he's a maverick, he still possesses an acute tenderness that will leave him exposed to his love interest. He likes his women smart and sexy. And when he's into you, his devotion knows no bounds.

He has the ability to rise to the top of any heap. But he lacks the responsibility that comes with power. He overspends lavishly and allows his friends to take advantage of his kindness. But they, like you, love being around him.

How to Sex the Aries Man

It takes a particular kind of woman to sexually satisfy the **Aries** man. She must be explicit, imaginative and boundless.
Satisfy his whims or else. He likes to ride bareback. He likes to take charge in the bedroom. At times, he can be a bit rough; overly aggressive. He likes to watch you groan, jerk, ouch, or pull away-so that he can grab you and pound you harder. It makes him sexually euphoric. He's full of surprises in the bedroom.

But remember, he likes to bring the pain. So he won't be shy about pulling out whips, chains or spikes. The **Aries** man can get really kinky too. He's definitely down for swinging. He's the kind of guy who will organize, dictate and take charge in an orgy.

The **Aries** man will ram his spear in every hole you've got, so have plenty of lubricants on stand by. He's an impulsive type of freaky lover who gets a rush from wild sex. If you can't comply with his demands, stay away from the **Aries** man. He'll drop you quick if you can't take his bossy, abrasive sex style.

*Aries men are most compatible with Sagittarius, Capricorn and Aquarius.

Finding Your Perfect Sexual Match by Lysa London

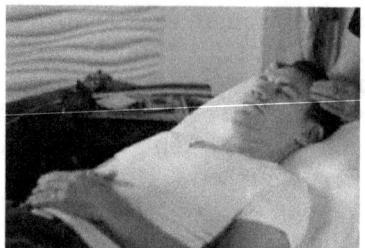

Massage his scalp and temple gently to get the ram worked up.

Finding Your Perfect Sexual Match by Lysa London

The Taurus Man

**Taurus is the Symbol of the Bull
(April 20-May 20)**

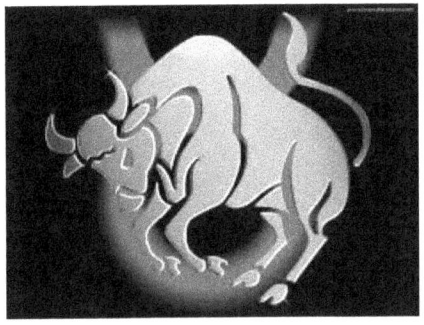

LADIES, the **Taurus** man doesn't give up on give in easily. He rarely stops until he gets what he wants. He's slow to rise but when he gets up, he's hell. Don't play games with the **Taurus** man. He gets pissed when he figures out your game.

He will become as stubborn as a mule when he doesn't want to do something. Arguing and badgering won't help you. If you're involved with a physical **Taurus**, you already know that he has no qualms putting his hands on a woman.

He likes to set the mood with wine and song. He likes nice things and takes care of them. He takes care to find the pleasure in what he likes. If he's at the club or bar he savors the top shelf liquors and wines. When its time to eat, he seeks out the best restaurants and cooks. If his woman does him right, hell always show his appreciation in different ways.

No woman is too good for him. He feels he deserves the best and intends to get it. He's comfortable in his manhood so don't expect fake or frivolous-he keeps it real. He's not a dunce with his money, so don't try to play him. Hell stroke you a check when he's good and ready.

He saves money with a purpose and a plan in mind. And when its time to make the big purchases hell be the one who pulls out a knot of money so big it can choke a horse. The **Taurus** man isn't afraid to get his hands dirty, so hard work doesn't faze him.

Remember, there are two types of male **Taurus**'. Type 1 beginning month **Taurus** can be adrenaline junkies who crave excitement. And type 2- ending month **Taurus**, are shrewder when approaching problems.

Your **Taurus** man has a serious jealousy streak. So if you break up, it's best to cut ties completely. His selfish nature forces him to go all in on everything; including love. Early month **Taurus'** are right now type of guys; pushing hard for what they want. They don't care who gets caught in the middle. Later month **Taurus'** are all over the place. They will go all the way around the hen house to get to the barn.

Not to be vulgar, but when the **Taurus** man smells pu**y, he's like a bull seeing red. He can become like an overprotective caveman daring anybody to come near you.

How to sex the Taurus Man

If you want to snag "Taurus the bull," be yourself. At a party **Taurus** will be the cool, stern guy holding up the wall, yet completely comfortable doing it. It may take a while for him to ask you out but when he does he's definitely interested. Or if you really want to impress him, cook him a great meal.

When it comes to sex the **Taurus** man is insatiable. He loves sex. And it doesn't take much to get him started. **Taurus** man is a sucker. He likes to suck toes, breasts, back and everything below your navel. He may use hot oils or honey to get the party stated.

Don't skimp out on the foreplay; he likes it. And if you need to, take an energy drink because **Taurus** man can go and go and go. And you don't have to always be your freshest with the **Taurus** man. Funky odors can often get him really excited.

The **Taurus** man is a real ass-man. He loves to touch, kiss, lick and enter the anus. He's one of the only signs attracted to unusual odors during sex. A woman's body odor may arouse him. He is also prone to sexual fetishes the majority of people find offensive. His anal fetish could also push him towards bi-sexuality, so be warned.

The Taurus man is most compatible with Cancer, Pisces and Libra.

Soft, slow kisses around the neck will get the party started with the Taurus man.

Finding Your Perfect Sexual Match by Lysa London

The Gemini Man

Gemini is the Symbol of the Twins
(May 21-June 20)

Ladies, the **Gemini** man is a rolling stone who likes to keep it moving. He doesn't waste time. He jumps from one thing to the next showing passion then suddenly; displeasure. He's often hiding his true feelings behind a wall of contradictions.

Finding Your Perfect Sexual Match by Lysa London

He's seldom on time but his smooth talking ways keep people from going off on him. He's smart and able to debate with the best of them. He's able to keep you off balanced with his big ideas. But he can be easily distracted by others.

He does his work but only in intervals, because something else always gets his attention. Don't get angry when the **Gemini** says one thing and does another. Try to understand, it's those twins battling inside him.

When women are near, he can become prideful with a huge ego. So his chauvinistic qualities are never far behind. To be his woman, you must not submit too easily. Push back a little before letting him savor his win over you. His ego likes to showcase his superior intellect over his woman.

The **Gemini** man may at times seem a bit flakey for not staying on task and running elsewhere. But this rolling stone is looking for something else, somewhere else. He'll leave a good job just when he was really fitting in, all because he'll get bored with the same routine.

Money doesn't stay in his pockets for long. He always seems to find a way to spend it all up. His childlike behavior can sometimes make him seem immature, but gambling, hanging out and good times are his universe. This man lives for the right now-tomorrow is exactly that; tomorrow.

Finding Your Perfect Sexual Match by Lysa London

If you want to catch a **Gemini**, look for the guy who fights against boredom and monotony. He will liven up your party by making people become more lucid and free flowing. He has a flair for the unusual.

If you go out, suggest someplace he's never been for your first date. Keep him guessing and you'll keep him. You must never become complaisant- never stop peaking his interest.
Stimulate his mind and his body will follow. Play the mysterious woman role. That will keep him guessing.

How to Sex the Gemini Man

Don't put stock in oral sex with the **Gemini** man. He can take it or leave it. He knows how to get you excited. His talent for the ladies can lead to your panties coming all the way off pretty fast. He knows what to say to get what he wants. He isn't shy about having sex in other places outside the home; cars, vans, offices, elevators, etc.

If it seems like your **Gemini** man is more interested in your sexual behavior and/ or his own dalliances don't be alarmed. The twins inside him like to watch themselves get down; even grading their performance.

He will gravitate towards a swinger lifestyle if you allow it. And will not hesitate to sex you while another woman watches. The **Gemini** male will get deep into sexual toys and devices to stimulate and heighten the sex.

Always remember, the **Gemini** represents duality. He may do something wild like pick up hookers just to spank them. He likes to experiment. Some are even pushed by their evil twin to cross dress and become sexually violent. Bi-sexuality is also an option if it involves new, freaky sex acts. More curious than a cat, he will push the boundaries of experimentation for gratification. If you want to sex the **Gemini** man, it's a safe bet the twins are going to be experimenting on you.

*Gemini Men are best compatible with Leo, Aries and Aquarius.

Suck his fingers and watch the Gemini nature rise.

Finding Your Perfect Sexual Match by Lysa London

The Cancer Man

Cancer is the Symbol of the Crab (June 21-July22)

Ladies, this water sign doesn't trust strangers- he watches them with a suspicious eye. So be careful how you approach and choose your words carefully. He may think you're trying to set him up. When he's up he's up, but when he's down he's down. The **Cancer** male has the energy to make you feel the same way he does.

Finding Your Perfect Sexual Match by Lysa London

Cancer man will protect his woman and to her he reveals his softer side. He loves hot women with beauty and brains; and they love him too. But once he falls for you, he becomes strict and rigid. When disagreements occur he tends to hold a lot inside. Don't bagger him about telling you what's wrong; hell come around when he's ready.

If you want to meet and date a Cancer man, tell him you have a problem that needs resolving. His analytical mind will come to the rescue. On a date, go to an ol' school concert with smooth jazz or something sultry. Don't talk about your ex unless he asks. He definitely doesn't want to hear about your old romances or sexual history.

If you're feeling sick or if you're feeling down he's a comforter. He'll rub your back, shoulders and feet. He'll even cook for you-if he's a man who knows his way around the kitchen. If you find a **Cancer** man who is a mama's boy, watch out, they are so laid back that they become lazy.

He'll take you to a nice restaurant but he'd prefer a home cooked meal. He studies human nature and is a master of words. He has the ability to get people excited; he stirs up their sleeping emotions with his ideas. He has a memory like an elephant and never forgets a face.

He's full of head strong opinions and wants you to adhere to his point of view. But he's also a good listener who will lend a hand to someone in need.

He's good with his money and you can even trust him with your money. He has the discipline to invest it wisely.

He's a good analytical thinker who exudes confidence and knows how to keep his mouth shut. But his secrets are going to be his. And his deepest ones he'll rarely, if ever, share.

Cancer men live in the past and are resistant to change. He's far more then just nostalgic, he actually wishes he could be "back in the day." But when he's into you, he's one of the most loyal signs of the zodiac. And he expects your complete fidelity.

He may have a tendency to be over confident with his woman. He's so sure that she will not cheat or betray him, he sometimes allows other men too close to her zone. You have to remind him, men will still be men and that you require his vigilance.

He looks for wife material in all his women but if it's not there, she becomes merely a friend with benefits. He's a stubborn character who doesn't like to lose or give up. He's smart and puts 100% into all of his endeavors.

Finding Your Perfect Sexual Match by Lysa London

How to Sex the Cancer Man

First of all, pucker-up and give him a big kiss. I'm talking about tonguing him down-French style. Second, pinch and squeeze his nipples, those are his hot spots. Third, lift his shirt and suck his nipples and his penis will become as stiff as a board. Gently stroke his chest during sex, too. He enjoys that.

The **Cancer** man likes to be in control of your body during sex. And that includes your tongue and mouth. Don't talk dirty to him. He'll get turned off. But if you like dirty talk with your sex, just ask him- he'll oblige.

During foreplay, stroke his penis while licking his testicles and he might orgasm then and there. Squeeze your breasts with his penis in-between. That's yet another sex secret of the **Cancer** man's sexual zodiac.

Finding Your Perfect Sexual Match by Lysa London

Cancer man wants to fulfill your needs. He's not a selfish lover. He works to make sure you both achieve orgasms. He has tenderness in his touch and seems to always know where you want him to put his magic fingers.

*Cancer males are most compatible with Virgo, Cancer, Taurus and sometimes Pisces.

**Suck the Cancer Man's nipples
And he becomes as hard as a rock!**

Finding Your Perfect Sexual Match by Lysa London

The Leo Man

Leo is the Symbol of the Lion (July 23-August 22)

Ladies, your Leo man likes to be seen. He likes to shine. All you have to do is take notice. Tell your **Leo** man that you find him absolutely fascinating. They love compliments. **Leo** man likes to know that you can't do without him. Having a good sense of humor is a big plus to catching a Leo because they like to laugh.

They like being where the excitement is. Don't be cheap or petty when entertaining the Leo man. He likes fashion and pizzazz, so don't skimp out on the extras. Throw a party and make a fuss over this. Talk about their raise, promotion or success. When seducing a Leo, think King or big boss, anything but simple and you can't go wrong.

Finding Your Perfect Sexual Match by Lysa London

Women are attracted to the **Leo** male. They're always checking him out and men hate on him. He likes the hot chicks but doesn't want them dressed like whores. Don't try to out shine him. He's the one who must be seen. He loves to bask in the sun; literally and figuratively. He likes being outside, because the sun is his God.

The **Leo** man loves sports because he is competitive. He knows how to turn a loss into a win. His outgoing nature will often find a way to grab attention from the victor. He likes nothing but the best. He has luxurious tastes. He's not going to half ass it. He will take a chance on anything.

Everybody likes **Leo** because he's a big spender who will take care of everything. He is a good friend who will go to leaps and bounds to protect his friends and loved ones. He is quite popular but he needs others to see him the way he sees himself. That's his vulnerability. He goes overboard to win people over. Compliments and praise can influence his decision making; leaving him vulnerable to manipulation.

His romantic inclinations can at times appear to be fickleness; but its not. He falls in and out of love because he loves romance. He doesn't like slutty women but will end up with slutty women because they know vanity is his weakness. But you get caught playing around with other men. The **Leo** man is very jealous. He'll beat you both down.

The **Leo** male takes a lackadaisical approach to work. If he's doing a job he doesn't like, hell let others handle the little things because he finds it tedious. And if he messes up, he'll just blame it on somebody else.

The showman in him likes the style, flash and pizzazz, not the concrete. He likes to have his way and refuses to listen to descending opinions. If at the losing end of an argument, don't worry, he'll bounce back in no time, ready for another challenge.

How to Sex the Male Leo

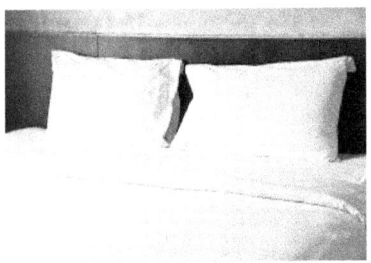

The **Leo** male loves women and he needs them like the rest of us need air. He loves the chase and the fun that comes with it. He is a sexual connoisseur. The rules of engagement (courtship) do not apply to him. He hates a tease, so don't make sexual promises you can't keep. But that doesn't mean spread your legs early.

Finding Your Perfect Sexual Match by Lysa London

You can keep his attention by playing hard to get. He already thinks every woman wants him; you have to at least play coy. He likes his woman submissive and timid in the bedroom so that he can control the sexual flow. So take orders and stroke his ego.

The **Leo** man wants to satisfy himself first, you second. Then he'll act like he's done you a favor. He has great stamina when it comes to having sex, but that doesn't mean he wants to **"hit it"** every night. But when you are having sex, let him know you're enjoying it. He likes to hear you call his name.

If you're in a relationship with a **Leo** man and you plan to withhold sex in order to control him; don't. He'll go elsewhere. And that's not what you want. He likes to control the bedroom, including his favorite position; doggy style.

He's not big on giving head, just receiving. So when he whips it out, get to work and act like you really enjoy it. Tell him how big or smooth his penis is; you'll unknowingly be hitting a home run. Don't be surprised if the **Leo** male is clean shaved around the penis area. He's trying to give his penis more appeal. So take notice.

The Leo man is most compatible with Aries, Gemini and Sagittarius.

Finding Your Perfect Sexual Match by Lysa London

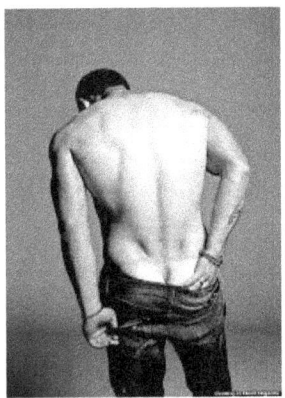

Tickle and stroke Leo's lower back and watch him become as hard as a rock.

The Virgo Man

Virgo is the symbol of the Virgin (August 23-September22)

LADIES: First, you need to know he's all about the money. And his interests are anything that will put money into his pockets. Virgo males like to know how much money you have because they hate to spend theirs. So don't be surprised when you meet the Virgo male and he keenly assesses how much you're worth.

Finding Your Perfect Sexual Match by Lysa London

They are practical and not whimsical with their money. His friendships are specific and refined. He doesn't like giving compliments so don't expect him to drool all over your new outfits but that doesn't mean he didn't notice.

The Virgo male like's routine. He will value exercise and nutrition; even on his day off. If you look carefully, you'll find most unmarried men are Virgos who choose work over romance. But they can create the illusion of a loving spouse.

They like all the other signs to view them in a good, positive light. They are non confrontational to passive. And it is only with someone close to him that he will reveal his true self... his true thoughts... his true mindset.

The Virgo Man has a strong sense of responsibility. They will perform their duties well. You can depend on him to stay on task; paying the mortgage, lights and car note. He has the preparedness of a Boy Scout, so it's hard to catch him off guard.

Don't expect to make the Virgo man your eye candy because he's not a fashion fiend. He has a no frills dress code. He's a homebody and hates to go out. But don't be late. The Virgo man abhors tardiness.

He doesn't lose his temper often; instead he becomes a fatherly protector over his woman. That makes a good friend and advisor. He's not the romantic type and can drag his feet for years before popping the big question.

The Virgo man likes a woman with class. But you'd better have some money to settle down with the Virgo male. He won't say I do unless it absolutely benefits him. He's tight on a dollar unless it's something he wants for himself. You can romanticize life with the Virgo male, but stability is what you'll get.

How to Sex the Virgo Man

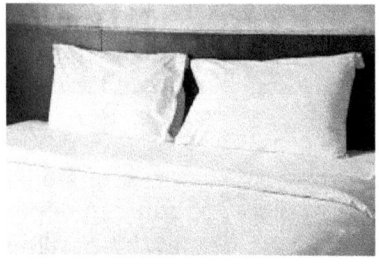

You will have to make the first move; first date and first kiss. If you want him to touch your breasts, you'll likely have to take his hands and literally place them there. He can be quite shy.

The Virgo man's foreplay can seem robotic and routine. But it's done more to please you then him. He's trying to get you excited. If you don't like it tell him how you do like it. But be careful. Don't be rude or crude. It doesn't take much for his penis to go soft.

Once the **Virgo** man gets warmed up, he'll go all out to please you. He's usually a missionary man, so you'll have to prompt him for more. Tell him how you want it. Be sexually aggressive if you please, **Virgo** man will accommodate.

Use your sweet, 'honey please' voice. He will accept and cater to your new positions as long as you're not too forceful. Treat him like a novice; guiding him down your sexual path. Rub his abs or stomach that gets him started.

On a harder note that must be discussed, the **Virgo** male can develop strange, sexual habits that you need to be aware of: Pornography and masturbation is the direction a lot of older **Virgo** males go.

At some point in the relationship, the **Virgo** male can become less interested in satisfying your sexual needs. The older the **Virgo**, the less interested in sex he can become.

In the meantime, a thirst for porn will develop which can lead to weirder, sexual appeasements; odd fetishes that will make him masturbate and get off.

He may not even care if you cheat because satisfying you is a thing of the past. He'll still notice you but doesn't want to sex you.

This sexual deviance can arrive with money hoarding and selfishness. He will become territorial to overcompensate for his lake of intimacy.

The Virgo man is most compatible with Taurus, Cancer and Capricorn.

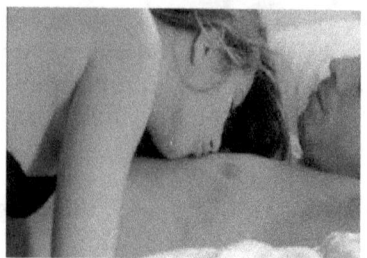

Put warm oil gently across his stomach
which should include your tongue and fingertips.

The Libra Man

Libra is the Symbol of the Scales
(Sept 23 –October 22)

Ladies, the **Libra** man is for peace and harmony. The scale of his nature makes him weigh the odds of everything. He's a very intuitive person who will rarely, if ever, fall for your deceptions and games. He hates to make a public spectacle of himself. So all that arguing in restaurants or making a jealous scene at the club that you use to do, **Libra** man will avoid drama and give you your walking papers.

He values the artistry in everyday things. If you're a good actress, poet or singer- he'll enjoy your work.

Finding Your Perfect Sexual Match by Lysa London

And if you're against the ropes, he'll have your back. He always seems to favor the underdog.

He's passionate about love, life and women. **Libra** man falls in love easily. In fact, he's quicker then most to walk down the isle. He'll say I do as long as you're not pushy. Just don't aggravate him with the arrangements. The **Libra** man is not a sucker. Don't expect him to be easily duped. Such an assumption will end your relationships.

The **Libra** man will go all out to satisfy his woman in bed. If you want it fast call him. If you like it nice and slow, whisper it in his ear. He's a fool for a sweet talking woman; tell him he's handsome and sexy and he becomes putty in your hands. A demanding woman can have him wrapped around her finger.

But you must stay out of other men's faces. **Libra** men "don't play that at all." And you may have to get rid of most of your guy friends, he's very territorial. He likes fashionable women with shoulder length hair and juicy lips.

If you're out to catch a **Libra** man think classy-not sluttish. Give him genuine compliments about the things you like or notice about him. Remember, he's good at seeing through phony people. If you're treating or going Dutch take him someplace nice, quiet and upscale to eat. And if he comes to your place for dinner, be sure that it's neat, clean orderly and stylish. He'll take notice and his scales will weigh you on what he sees.

Finding Your Perfect Sexual Match by Lysa London

How to Sex the Libra Man

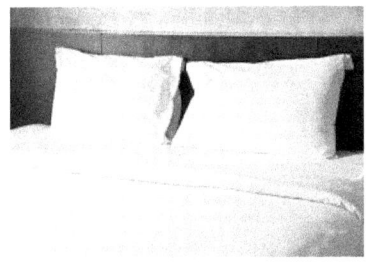

Unfortunately, your **Libra** man is not the monogamous sign. Most of his relationships are casual; hence the reason why **Libra** men juggle women. And the ladies like his many charms; especially when it involves sex.

When it comes to the bedroom, tell the **Libra** man what you want and he'll comply. He's one of the few signs who'll go out of his way to make sure you're satisfied. He's a slow starter but don't push him or he'll clam right on up. Allow him to set the pace. Sex with him is a process- you'll have to sit back and enjoy. He doesn't like being commanded around the bedroom. He'll actually do whatever you say, if you say it soft and gently-let him take his sweet time.

The **Libra** man is not by nature rough. So if you like to be rammed and jammed he's not the one for you.

Finding Your Perfect Sexual Match by Lysa London

Your **Libra** likes to explore your body using all out foreplay and passion.
There's no part of your body his tongue, lips or fingers won't enter. He'll make you tremble with delight.

The **Libra** likes to watch. Don't be surprised if you find mirrors over his bed or a camera hidden somewhere. Women are often in hot pursuit of the **Libra** man because he's very appealing. He's dirty in a clean way.

But be warned, many **Libra** men easily catch the eye of homosexual males as well. Some resist, others dive on in- meaning some of them go both ways. He likes watching porno flicks and masturbating to whatever scene suits his fantasy.

He can go periods of time without asking you for sex- but when the feeling hits; he really wants to get super freaky. If you let the **Libra** man have his way with you prepare yourself for those multiple orgasms.

Libra men are most compatible with Leo, Gemini and Aquarius.

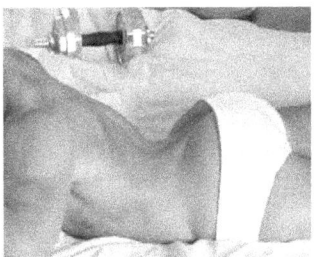

***Slap his ass before and during sex.
It drives the Libra man crazy.***

Finding Your Perfect Sexual Match by Lysa London

The Scorpio Man

Scorpio is the Symbol of the Scorpion (October 23-November 21)

Ladies, the first thing you should know is that the **Scorpio** man thinks with his dick. He will do anything to satisfy his nature and could care less about the aftermath. He will go far and wide to get laid if there's risk involved. The **Scorpio** man exudes a strong sexual energy that pulls women in. He also has an interesting charisma that people like.

Women have to be on guard because the **Scorpio mojo** is so strong females often get caught up in it before they even know what happened. The **Scorpio** man will not warn you that drama may come with his lustful behavior because he's usually thinking with the little head.

Finding Your Perfect Sexual Match by Lysa London

The **Scorpio** man can be your greatest lover or your worst sexual experience in life. When he has his sights on you, he's hard to slow down; and won't stop 'til he gets it. Once the **Scorpio** has been told 'no' enough times by you, he will then try to take it- watch out!

Scorpio has a memory like an elephant, so if you cross him, he will never forget. If you treat him like gold, he wont forget that either. He usually has turbulent relationships with everybody. And he's always ready for a fist fight. If you've ever been in a conflict with a **Scorpio** man, then you already know that he is strong willed, determined and dogged. He is uncompromising and pitiless.

He is an emotional Wildman who rarely shows weakness and doesn't tolerate weak friends. He will go all in on drinking and drugging. But once that phase passes, he's done. His strong resolve keeps him steady. **Scorpio** man likes to work and doesn't mind going it alone. He's a maverick when it comes to self employment. He's not a dunce with his money, so don't try to clown him. His temper is furious.

The **Scorpio** man expects nothing but total compliance. His needs come first. He approaches sex with total abandon and the need for control. He'll go after the hottest chick around-even the woman who belongs to somebody else. Don't get caught cheating on a **Scorpio** man. He'll whip both of your asses ...or worse!

If you want to catch a **Scorpio** wear sexy clothes, super tight jeans and a low cut blouse. **Scorpio** is insightful and can see what you're hiding. But he also demands all your attention. Show him concentrated affection and you're in there. He'll get jealous of whom- ever is taking your attention away from him. That includes a heavy workload.

You'll rarely, if ever win an argument with your **Scorpio** man. He's got to always be right. **Scorpio** wants to entertain you at home. So suggest home cooked meals and candlelight dinner with wine. And when you go out to dinner, suggest sea food; one of **Scorpio's** favorite. Remember, **Scorpio** is a-know- it all, so don't ruffle his feathers with contradictions or you'll lose him for sure. He can't stand a woman with a sassy mouth.

How to Sex the Scorpio Man

Finding Your Perfect Sexual Match by Lysa London

The **Scorpio** is the type of sexual beast every woman wants in her bed. He comes to play and he delivers in spades. He doesn't slack off. He goes straight to work. He kisses hard and licks everything down the middle. He's great at oral sex, too. He likes giving a woman multiple orgasms.

He may spank you, bite your ass and squeeze your nipples when he's excited. He completely controls the sex and dominates his woman. His mind believes that women like it rough. He loves receiving oral sex. He loves receiving oral sex in the shower and/or hot tub. This water sign likes seeing you wet and dripping; fresh out of the shower or bath; tell him to take you.

Scorpio is insatiable; wanting more and more...seconds and thirds. So you better eat your wheaties. He hates using a condom and really doesn't care if you get pregnant. The **Scorpio** man can get pretty freaky with objects and oils; anything to make it unforgettable. But be careful. He's prone to sadism; bind, torture, beat. To a lot of the **Scorpio** men- pain means pleasure.

*Scorpio male is most compatible with Cancer, Capricorn and Pisces.

Finding Your Perfect Sexual Match by Lysa London

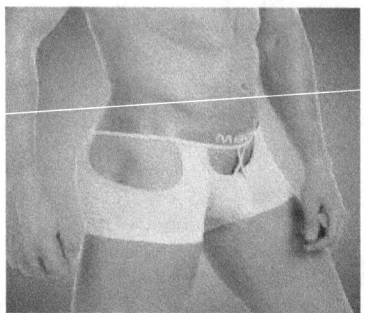

Kiss and lick the head of your Scorpio's Penis and watch him go buck wild!

Finding Your Perfect Sexual Match by Lysa London

The Sagittarius Man

Sagittarius is the Symbol of the Archer (November 22-December 21)

Ladies, when you meet the **Sagittarius** man you'll feel like you're the only two in the room. He overwhelms you with flattery and charisma. But he'll do the same to the next chic. He is a natural flirt whether you're married, single or with child. He likes hot women and intends to impress them. He goes all out too; texts, calls and c-mails. The **Sagittarian** man overwhelms you with his attentiveness and preferential treatment.

Finding Your Perfect Sexual Match by Lysa London

He's always looking for the perfect love and is usually disappointed. But when it comes near, he's afraid, and he may self sabotage. He's fond of "no strings attached", relationships because they don't require commitment; therefore, they don't accompany disappointment. This man does expect your word to be your bond. It is when you fall short on these expectations he will not trust you at all.

He's an up front type of guy who will say what's on his mind and he's trust worthy and capable. He likes everything on point and precise. **Sagittarian** males highly regard your truth; state your intention and he will quickly let you know whether it fits into the scheme of his lifestyle.

He is a big spender who will give you nice things. He doesn't like crowds but will prefer a walk on the beach as it poses to be a more intimate setting. He loves to hop on a plane and become spontaneous about the endeavors he will take on and learn from along the way.

These experiences help to shape his black and white character traits. All the future advice he will give will be solely based on personal experience in which he will ascertain as "the rule." He will enthrall you by helping to make your dreams come true; whatever it is that you truly have your mind set on-he'll work to make it happen- no matter what the price.

If you want to catch a **Sagittarius** man wear a sexy dress that exposes your legs. He's an avid leg man so make sure that your legs are nicely shaved and oiled. That's an extreme turn-on.

He doesn't like quiet or shy women. He prefers upbeat women who can appreciate his stories and jokes. I hope you like fishing and camping because he does. Any fun activity that takes place outside, **Sagittarius** men usually enjoy. He hates being cooped up in the house. Go see some stand-up comedy or a stage play.

How to Sex the Sagittarius Man

The **Sagittarius** man "loves women." He's a hopeless romantic. He has a picture of what a great romance looks like and that is what he searches for in the arms of women.

In the bedroom he can literally come and go in no time and there will be no cuddling. But if you like it often, he's your guy. He's one of the few signs who'll want to have sex every night. But be careful, he has the stamina to be doing you and be juggling a couple of side dishes as well!

Finding Your Perfect Sexual Match by Lysa London

This persuasive sign has the gift of gab and will sooner or later convenience you to let him enter the back door (anal). He's good with his mouth and knows where to put it. One of his sexual fetishes is putting his penis between your breasts while you sandwich his penis until he ejaculates.

He likes a woman in high heels and stockings. In fact, keep them on sometimes when you're having sex. Use rubbing oils, scented oils and sex oils.

He likes sexy but not trashy. And often when a woman tells him yes, he's in such a rush, he'll finish before she even gets warmed up. But if you're itching to try something different, something hot and erotic, just whisper it to your **Sagittarius** man and he'll oblige. And be warned; he'll put his tongue and fingers everywhere during sex, so be ready.

*The Sagittarius man is most compatible with Aquarius, Libra, Leo, and sometimes Aries- if they click in the bedroom.

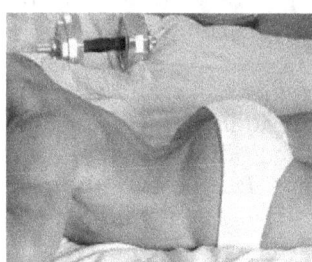

Massage his lower back, butt and thighs with warm oil and he'll heat up every time.

Finding Your Perfect Sexual Match by Lysa London

The Capricorn Man

Capricorn is the Symbol of the Goat
(December 22- January 19)

Ladies, the **Capricorn** man is a determined man. He will keep trying to get into your panties again and again and again. This man breathes love and he must have it. He is a lustful man who believes that he can bring the freak out of any woman. He's ruthless when it comes to sex. His number one hobby is manipulating young girls.

His impatience is well known so good luck trying to make him wait. He doesn't play games so don't call him up late at night unless you intend to get down. Although his passion runs deep, a true **Capricorn** is not a cheating sign. If you tell him you love him and immediately commit, so will he.

If you want to catch a **Capricorn** you have to keep it 100 percent real. They can tell when you're running game. He likes a woman who has a good head on her shoulders. But if you don't know about religion or politics, don't pretend. Brush up on current events. Show him you can cook, then ply him with good food, wine and intelligent conversation.

He can be incorrigible- having sex multiple times all over the house. When have retired from sex, **Capricorn** man won't slow down until he's dead. Even without Viagra, **Capricorn** is always nudging you in the middle of the night.

He loves a woman who makes money and can keep his secrets. But you have to be a team. The demanding, chauvinistic **Capricorn** will reward your efforts; sexually and financially.

He has a one tack mind- like a horse with blinders seeing nothing but the finish line. Or some may call it a dog with a bone. **Capricorns** are usually bosses who climb the ladder of success then look out for those who helped him along the way. If he's knocked down he gets back up. Never count him out.

How to Sex the Capricorn Man

With him, love is physical. And when he's ready for sex, saying no is unacceptable. It will serve you best to learn his sexual likes and dislikes fast; he expects nothing less. **Capricorn** *puts in the work. He doesn't stop until you get enough; orgasm. He likes to set the mood; soft lights and baby making music. He's in charge in the bedroom so let him have his way.*

He likes to see you strip, tease and grind. It arouses him. He's also excited by blindfolds and gags. It gives him the fantasy of taking it. But you've got to know your man. If you go too deep down that rabbit hole- you may not return. It could lead to sadomasochism.

When the **Capricorn** *man is having sex he'll satisfy you which satisfies his ego. Keep in mind, during sex his primary concern is self enjoyment. And if it takes hurting you to achieve this euphoria he won't mind.*

The **Capricorn** *man, like the Taurus, are ass men; quick to enter the back door. They'll play all kinds of anal games which include tossing your salad to straight up paddling that ass. Be ready!*

*Capricorn Male is most compatible with Scorpio, Pisces and Taurus

Finding Your Perfect Sexual Match by Lysa London

Rub your breasts all over your Capricorn man's body and watch him explode with passion.

Section 2

A Man's Astrological Guide to Love, Sex and Intimacy

Aquarius...58

Pisces...62

Aries...66

Taurus...70

Gemini...74

Cancer...78

Leo...82

Virgo...86

Libra...90

Scorpio...93

Sagittarius...97

Capricorn...101

The Aquarius Woman

Aquarius is the Symbol
of the Water Bearer
(January 20-February 18)

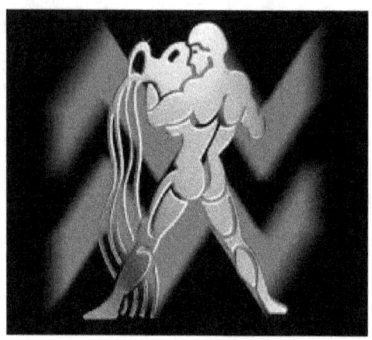

Sometimes thought of as snobbish or bougie, the **Aquarius** woman has a low tolerance for rude or crude. She sets the bar high when it comes to relationships. She must be treated like a lady. If you're merely looking to get laid, find another sign. She doesn't consider that respectful.

She's a smart people person who likes to socialize. She's straight forward and an open book to the man she likes. She prides herself on being an uncertified therapist to those in need; always doling out advice like a prescription.

She doesn't mind hard work; blue collar or white. But it can't be boring. It must be challenging. She was born with a deeply sympathetic nature. She likes to help the underprivileged because she's a giver and not a taker.

Aquarius women often believe in astrology and magic. She will indulge deeply in both. She loves men and insists on having a mate; not multiple or simultaneous lovers. If she puts on something new, take notice. If she gets her hair done, tell her it looks great. If she stands in front of you naked, tell her she's got a banging body. She needs to know that you see and appreciate her efforts.

She keeps things clean and tidy; at work and at home. She can sometimes over-indulge in creature comforts-silk sheets and $200.00 comforters. She seeks comfort ability, not necessarily luxury.

To catch an **Aquarius** woman be some place fun. She'll show up. They like social gatherings like cookouts, barbecues, card parties, fundraisers, etc. People are drawn to their interesting conversations. Don't be shy about asking her out. She likes an assertive man.

On your first date take her some place fun but artful; like a talent show or a state of the art museum. But avoid the same old run-in-the-mill movies or nightclub. Aquarius woman is a private person- ***"so don't be all up in her business."*** Let the evening flow and try to make a connection.

How to Sex the Aquarius Woman

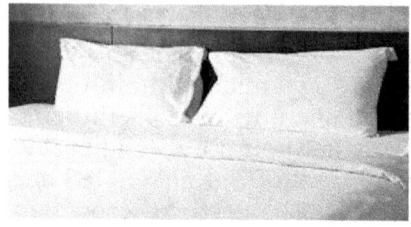

Men, you have to let the **Aquarius** woman warm up first. Think romantic, not aggressive. But once you get her going, she's down for whatever. She'll do freaky positions and party all night long if that's what her man wants. Tell her you're into the super-freaky and she'll do it just to make you happy.

The **Aquarius** woman tends to put her man's sexual needs and gratification ahead of her own. She's so anxious to please you it often borders desperation. If you're having trouble getting hard she'll give you oral until you do. If your Viagra hasn't kicked in, she'll give you oral until it does. If you're long winded, she'll let you keep stroking until you orgasm.

Finding Your Perfect Sexual Match by Lysa London

She doesn't mind semen anywhere you put it; face, lips, hair, breasts, back, etc. And yes, she'll do anal too. With her, it's all about making the man happy.

Honestly, the **Aquarius** woman is the one sign you stand a better then average chance of getting what's called "sympathy pu**y." If you're crying on her shoulder, well, you just might get lucky. Men are sometimes able to toy with her heartstrings because the 'water bearer' can feel their pain.

Lonely, old men and lonely, lesbian women are sometimes able to play on her sympathetic nature and willingness to give them her body to make them feel better.

*Aquarius women are most compatible with Libra, Sagittarius, and Gemini.

Rub warm oil very gently on her calves and ankles to get her hot.

Finding Your Perfect Sexual Match by Lysa London

The Pisces Woman

Pisces is the Symbol of the Two Fish
(February 19-March 20)

If you are the man she feels she needs in her life, she will physically and mentally seduce you. She knows the art of seduction and plays that game well. She's often in a relationship with a soft spoken, gentleman with the reliable job that she can control. But deep down, she dreams about the hip-hop alpha male that will deliver passion and sex- a change from the mundane.

Sometimes her allure is too seductive, causing the crazies that she doesn't want, to come out of the woodwork. Careful, don't make her get a restraining order! When needed, she knows exactly how to become whatever she thinks a man wants. She can play the damsel in distress or the school girl looking for her teacher.

She has no problem using her body to get what she wants while giving men what they need. The planet Neptune is what controls her. Her mysterious ways hold men captive along with her sexy, womanly charms. If she begins to act insecure, it's due to old baggage from past relationships. She needs to know that you love her, so tell her often.

She's not aggressive at work or schemes to get her supervisor's job. She will accept the added responsibility but won't battle co-workers for the throne. Many **Pisces** women would prefer to sleep their way to the top.

Pisces women are easily hurt by harsh or mean-spirited words. They are even more sensitive then the crab sign. The Cancer can read you, but **Pisces** can sense your pain, hurt or despair. Her powers of perception lean more towards a sixth sense or clairvoyance.

She knows how to make a man happy at home. Her nurturing nature provides excellent mothering skills and good wife material. But men that she is incompatible with often end up in her bed and in her life. These relationships are toxic for the **Pisces** woman. The pressure can become unbearable; causing unusual, unstable actions.

She's not good with money. She sometimes will spend her last dollar on things most people will consider frivolous. She may even dig into her light bill money to buy gifts for others. She has a knack for choosing men that pull opposite to her nature. She will see the good in people, who actually don't have much good in them at all; at least not towards her. If she's able to combine the image of the man she has pictured in her head with the man that's standing in front of her; it's a winning relationship. Listen carefully to what she wants.

To catch a **Pisces** woman appeal to her artistic nature. If she likes to draw, talk about art. If she's into hip-hop, ask her about her favorite rapper. Take her to a concert. You can also talk to her about spirituality but let her do most of the talking.

Take her to a quiet restaurant; maybe something overlooking the water. After all, she is a **Pisces**. Suggest the beach or a one day cruise. If you take her to your place hide the liquor; she can't handle it. Either way, be strong, confident and sure. She likes a protector.

Finding Your Perfect Sexual Match by Lysa London

How to Sex the Pisces Woman

She can get pretty hot, really quickly. If she's reading a steamy, adult, fiction novel; get ready. If she's watching a torrid love scene on TV; get ready. She enjoys real action in the bedroom. And she's eager to satisfy the man. She enjoys foreplay just as much as intercourse. And she's willing to try all kinds of freaky things too. If she knows what you like sexually, she'll try to push that envelope even further, to enhance your pleasure even more.

The closer she gets to her monthly cycle, the hornier the **Pisces** woman will become. If you are her man, this will be super exciting for you because that's when you can bring the freak out of her. She likes giving oral sex and goes beyond the norm; licking, tasting and teasing your body in all the right places

Out of all the signs the **Pisces** woman will say yes to anal sex faster then any other sign. It's mostly because she'll do anything to please her man. If it gets him off she'll do it. You can blindfold her, tie her up, tie her down and paddle her butt until she turns red; she'll oblige that fetish. Perhaps you're the one who wants his rear end spanked; she's your girl. Leather, whips, chains, spikes, dildoes or lace panties, your wish is her command. If she's your sex partner, satisfaction is guaranteed!

***Pisces women are most compatible with Scorpio, Cancer, Capricorn and sometimes Aries.**

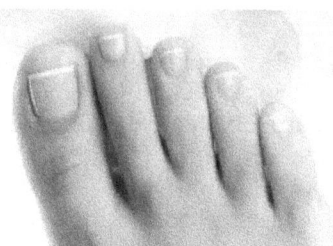

Sucking her toes is her weakness. But I'd Advise you to wash them first.

The Aries Woman

Aries is the Symbol of the Ram
(March 21-April19)

ARIES

Men, the **Aries** female is a tough nut to crack. She has a public face and a private face that rarely meet. She is literally all over the place because she is a restless spirit who often has a reckless mouth. She can be very attitudinal and brash.

Her quick temper spares no one nor will she sparse her words. When she's hyped up, she won't calm down until she knocks somebody out. The **Aries** woman is opinionated and bossy. To challenge her, your will must be stronger.

She is a romantic who loves being in love with a man. She can often remind you of a personal trainer; pushing you to enjoy life. Men are attracted to her outgoing personality.

Finding Your Perfect Sexual Match by Lysa London

She takes pride in her appearance; especially her body. She tries hard to maintain a sexy physique. And she likes to sleep naked, too. If you want to make an impression notice her body and give her realistic compliments; maybe how nice her clothes accentuate her body.

To catch an **Aries** woman go where the action is; NASCAR, football games, Casino, etc. You must have interesting conversation about your future plans or big ideas; no small talk-real talk. Be on time and don't be phony or pretentious. She hates an arrogant man. Your ego will clash with hers. Play the latest music, upbeat and happening.

If you pursue this woman, understand that you are second in command. She's the president and you're the vice. **Aries** women throw caution to wind which also encompasses their pocketbooks. She spends today and worries about tomorrow-some other time. She is an optimistic sign who gets better with age.

Her quick temper defies logical judgment which makes her make brash decisions. Your arguments will be intense- hence the term **"fighting like cats and dogs."** But She really sulks after a breakup because she hates being without her man.

Make sure that you're compatible before you pursue the **Aries** woman. She is indeed a wildcat. A hundred and fifty years ago she would've been a cowgirl. It's hard for the average guy to get the ***Aries*** woman out of his system. Her sexual dalliances and fetishes are some of the wildest of all the signs; and a lot of the male signs love it.

How to Sex the Aries Woman

When she's ready to have sex, she's ready to have sex- so don't be a lame lay or she'll chew you up and spit you out. She loves to have sex and her passions run deep. An **Aries** woman will have sex anywhere she pleases. If you're a take charge in the bedroom-type of guy, do it right or shell take over and your ego may never recover.

If you can't please her or tame her sexual appetite, she'll go elsewhere; plain and simple. She's a rider. She likes being on top; mostly to control the flow. Remember, she's a wildcat in bed as well as life.

If she's sexually attracted to a man, she's on him like the feds. Put a mirror next to the bed, too. She loves to look at herself; even during sex. And get some alcohol wipes because she's going to scratch your back and bite you.

When she's hot there's nothing sexually she won't try because she becomes overwhelmed with passion. Remember, she hates being bored. This can cause her to push the envelope towards dominatrix behavior.

She'll get off by beating you with a paddle or belt. Your pain will become her pleasure. If this was high school she'd be voted most likely to blindfold and handcuff her man. The **Aries** woman is the number one sign who'll stick a dildo in a man then slap him if he screams.

She likes wearing sexually, arousing undergarments and costumes to make her lover crave her even more. She's got plenty of energy too, so you better eat your Wheaties or gulp down an energy drink before you even think about diving onto an **Aries** woman.

*Aries women are most compatible with Sagittarius, Pisces, Aquarius, and sometimes Leo

Nibble or blow into her
ear to get her juices flowing.

The Taurus Woman

Taurus is the Symbol of the Bull
(April 20-May 20)

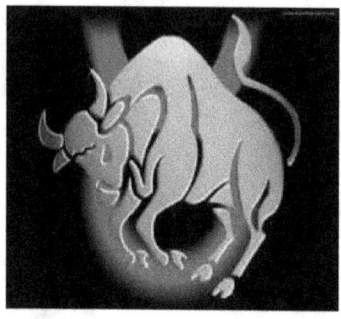

Men, she knows how to attract you. She knows what you like. When she bats her eyes, smiles or walks, the **Taurus** woman exudes sex. Men find her sexual energy hard to resist. She uses strong intuition when choosing a man and a sex partner.

Once she gets her man, there will be absolutely no sharing. She will demand her time and attention from you and your eyes better stay in your head. Or she will straight cuss you out. She's ardent about what she wants and isn't afraid to vocalize it. And believe me when she goes off, you're going to wish you'd given in sooner.

Finding Your Perfect Sexual Match by Lysa London

If she catches you cheating, be prepared for war! I'm talking about throwing blows. She'll never forgive and forget. On her nurturing side she is very soft and attentive; as she is ruled by the planet Venus, her affections will be strong. But keep it 100- as they say, because she's good at detecting liars and phonies.

The **Taurus** woman is often underestimated because she doesn't display the outward intellect of other signs. She relies mostly on her instincts for guidance. She's not awe struck but takes love and sex together. The young **Taurus** woman is eager and trainable. The first man who teaches her about love and sex can often win her heart. But afterwards the bar for the next suitor will be set specifically to her precision. Her man must satisfy her sexual needs and desires because if he doesn't, she'll most definitely go elsewhere.

She likes to dress nice but not flashy. She's practical, but loves her sentimental jewelry and tattoos; the gold necklace that her sister or best friend gave her. She likes nice things and knows how to take care of the gifts men bestow upon her. The man who 'makes it rain' has a special place in her heart.

But be careful. When **Taurus** women are happy-go-lucky in love they become complacent. She stops watching her figure and stops wearing those nice outfits she had on when you first met her. She's a bit shy in public so don't expect public displays of affection. Don't underestimate her either, although you may not think so, she has fortitude; real push power.

Oh, and just so you'd know. She doesn't like moist, soft spoken or metro-sexual men who get manicures and pedicures every week. No, only alpha males need apply.

How to Sex the Taurus Woman

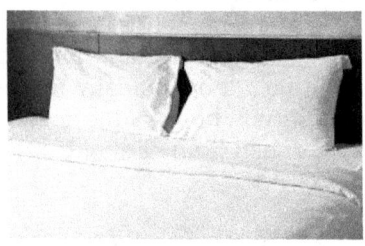

For her, the mood has to be right. Use music, incense, flowers, oils, candles or whatever it takes to set that mood. Make her comfortable. The bedroom is her layer; your place or hers. And she'll expect nothing but a stellar performance from you. Set the stage and you will be well rewarded.

She'll go that extra mile to please you sexually, if you're the man she desires. One **Taurus** woman told me she went out of her way to give a guy she hadn't long been dating the best oral sex he'd ever had. When I asked her why, she said "I wanted to make him my man." Yet another Taurus told me she milked all her ex-husbands prostates while she was performing oral sex. "That's why my relationships lasted so long," she smiled.

Most **Taurus** women have soft, smooth skin and luscious breasts. It's one of their identifying traits. When you rub, caress or kiss her breasts and nipples, be very gentle. And for God's sake no ashy, rough or calice hands; she hates that. Rub some lotion or Vaseline on your rough hands before you even think about touching her. She's into role play so why not suggest a little 'school girl/teacher' scenario to enhance your foreplay before the main course?

She likes a man who can offer her security and stability. She has a strong sexual drive that increases with the introduction of a man with means. Sometimes a sex addiction can occur if her needs are not met. That simply means that men with money and offering her sexual gratification at the same time, can rule the day.

Her fetishes as an older woman will vary but can range from getting aroused by your sweaty work shirt to getting turned on by your musty balls. She loves to receive oral sex; some have even become obsessed. If she's not careful her love for oral sex can lead her straight into the arms of a woman. Some aging **Taurus** women's aphrodisiac involves urine; watch it!

Taurus Women Are Most Compatible With Pisces, Libra and Cancer.

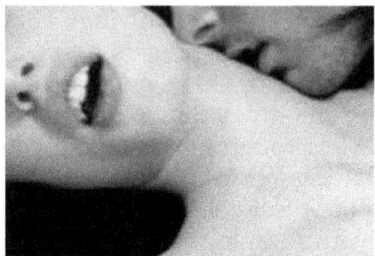

Taurus woman's neck is her sweet Spot. Soft kisses and gentle fingers makes her heat up.

Finding Your Perfect Sexual Match by Lysa London

The Gemini Woman

Gemini is the Symbol of the (May 21-June 20)

Men, the song "I'm Every Woman" had to be written about the **Gemini** female. She has the allure of mystery and intrigue. Then when you talk to her, she's charming, sharp, engaging and fun to chat with. She's often a walking therapist listening to problems and dosing out advice. People come to her with situations and she listens with support and empathy.

She can be pretty impulsive and go off half cocked without waiting for all the facts. Sometimes it's hard for her to stay focused. She can be all over the place; starting a new task before completing the last. She

Finding Your Perfect Sexual Match by Lysa London

can be happy and bubbly or quick tempered and really sad; all with- in the same two minutes.

She likes to work and make money and she wants a man who is as smart as she is. She's a good friend and confidant. But when she's young, **Gemini** women will have a lot of guy friends, and will play the field with the ones she finds interesting.

She can get a wild hair up her ass and won't sit still. She likes to change her scenery often; different restaurants, cars, even residences. This also applies to men. She'll try to fix up or change a man as it suits her.

Her sexy persona allows her seductive powers. She'll even use them for financial gain. And her conscience would not bother her at all. Be careful, a **Gemini** woman can draw you into her like a magnet against metal. One thing you can count on is the **Gemini** woman keeping you on your toes.

To catch a **Gemini** woman, you must be positive, upbeat and energetic. She likes mystery too; so you must become her mystery man and not the motor-mouth who tells all his business.

When you meet her it's like talking to an old friend and confidant; easy to talk to. She's telling you about crazy experiences in life and with people.

She's no stick in the mud and can party hard. If you take her to a club or a house party, make sure that's it's not whack. Don't take her anyplace boring or routine.

How to Sex the Gemini Woman

First and foremost, take your time. I'm not talking about how fast you stroke; I'm talking about not rushing her. She likes to enjoy sex without interruption. And don't say anything stupid because she can change her mind- like that. She likes the built up of foreplay and anticipation.

She likes to experiment, too. And her experimentations can go from the freaky to the crazy. She could care less what you or anybody else thinks about her sexual appetite or behavior. The twins inside the **Gemini** woman can often get her involved with women and play the male role in those relationships.

Finding Your Perfect Sexual Match by Lysa London

She favors using both hands during sex. For example; while giving you oral sex she may insert her finger into your anus. Or while performing oral sex she may play with your balls.

Out of all the zodiac signs, **Gemini** women are usually the most sexually active. And she'll have sex any place that suits her fancy. She sometimes plays punishment games with her men; pinching or digging her nails into his back.

Don't be surprised if she wants to mount you when you've just finished cutting the grass or chopping wood; let her. It doesn't matter if your balls are musty. She's prone to fetishes that can include your manly, musty smell.

*The Gemini Woman is most compatible with Leo, Aquarius and Aries.

Your lips rubbing ever so gently across the hands, arms and shoulders of your Gemini woman lights her fire.

Finding Your Perfect Sexual Match by Lysa London

The Cancer Woman

Cancer is the Symbol of the Crab
(June 21-July 22)

She is ruled by the moon. She's emotional and needs her friends. And she doesn't like you talking shit about her either; so watch your mouth. Just like her male counterpart, she has a memory like an elephant. She won't forget one single lie you've told nor how many times you've looked at some other woman's butt.

This history buff loves old movies and books. She likes to read about decades gone by and gentlemen who held the door for a lady. She has a keen eye for furniture, clothes, style and retro. She can cook her butt off too and likes to make certain everyone around her gets enough to eat. She's diligent at work and careful at play.

She likes being prepared and hates being caught off guard. She's thrifty and likes to save. And that includes your secrets. You can confide in her and count on her complete discretion. She is staunchly loyal to her man and he had better give her the attention she deserves. She likes the tender, emotional and attentive man. She doesn't like bossy, controlling, possessive or worrisome guys.

She's the quiet, reserved girl next door that most men want. She requires long term love and stability in a mate. The Cancer woman is fiercely loyal; the number one cheerleader and defender of her man. She's not down for just sex and go. She requires more. But if she's your woman, she'll give you all the freak nasty sex that you desire.

To catch a Cancer woman spark up a conversation about current events. Ask her about an upcoming election or ask her to attend an upcoming event. And do something to appeal to her nurturing nature. She likes soft music, slow jams, jazz or symphony.

Don't talk about your ex-girlfriends. Don't brag about money or your job; keep it simple. She's sensitive, so watch your mouth and your tone. Quiet evenings, moonlight walks on the beach or a music festival are good times.

Finding Your Perfect Sexual Match by Lysa London

How to Sex the Cancer Woman

At first, she may seem scared and reserved. So, she's definitely not going to make the first move. You must encourage her to relax, let go and feel free to be herself. Remember, this water sign is sensitive, so if you say something stupid or come off as too cocky, you're not getting laid. But if you're slow and gentle, she will give in to you. Don't push too hard and don't be too rough.

Once you get her comfortable, she's fantastic in bed. To achieve this make sure she's in safe and comfortable surroundings and that she knows you're really into her. Once she gets naked, take care to notice her hair, how good she smells and her luscious booty.

She will gladly give you oral sex. She loves to touch, feel and caress your penis and balls. She may pour something sweet on your package and lick it off. If she's too shy, you get the cool-aid yourself. She likes it from behind; face down-ass up. Or flat on her stomach where the man can enter her vagina from behind while grinding against her booty.

Keep an eye on your Cancer woman. All the Cancer women, who move outside of their normal sexual paradigm, can put themselves in extreme sexual circumstances. They will turn to men half their own age or younger; and don't rule out women either.

*Cancer women are most compatible with Taurus, Virgo Scorpio, and sometimes Pisces.

Tongue kiss her then lick and squeeze her nipples. That's what makes the Cancerian woman super horny!

The Leo Woman

Leo is the Symbol of the Lion
(July 23-August 22)

Men, the **Leo** woman likes to shine and she does it well. She likes the gaze in men's eyes when they marvel at her beauty. She likes to feel their lust before telling them 'no.' She demands exclusivity from her man. But she holds herself to a different standard. In other words; do as I say but not as I do.

The **Leo** woman is the most popular of the zodiac signs. She's a bossy chick who really loves herself. She is impulsive and flirtatious but doesn't chase men. She is often shallow and hard to pin down when it comes to commitment. In a long term relationship she can become complacent in the bedroom. This makes her man equally complacent. That's when things become stale and her feelings grow cold.

Finding Your Perfect Sexual Match by Lysa London

She will stay true to the man who loves her unless he screws up. When things go wrong she seldom shoulders the blame. This lioness can be a drama queen and at times her own worst enemy. She thinks the drama in her relationships occurs because she is so moral; however, her bossiness can sometimes cause the rift.

She loves to spend money on nice things and her man had better spend his money too. She likes getting her hair and nails done as well as buys that outfit she sees in Macy's store window. She likes to dress sexy; even provocative.

She's a colorful woman who loves to change the furniture around and invite friends over for a fancy party. In a party setting the **Leo** woman garners the attention of the men; even while their wives are visibly watching. This feline maintains the attention of many.

If you're her man always remind her that she's number one; your beauty with brains- queen. She likes to laugh and have fun. She can have quite the imagination and doesn't mind taking chances. Her demanding persona can sometimes make her that hard to deal with boss or co-worker. She likes to travel and can't stand being bored; anything but mundane. She's usually in a good mood, filled with an optimistic charm that will put you in a very pleasant mood too.

If you want to trap a lion; notice her. I mean really notice her smooth, unique persona. Use plenty of compliments. Show her you're willing to "do what you're told." Remember, she likes to laugh, so take her to see a romantic comedy or stand-up comedy.

Spend that money and splurge on what she wants. **Leo** doesn't do cheap or petty. She believes she deserves it all. Over dinner, talk about her for a while- her likes and dislikes; her hair, her nails, her cooking, her hobbies or talents. Just make sure it's flattering. If she decides to give you some, don't go to cheap hotels or your mama's house. It has to go down someplace comfortable to her and be to some degree, impressive.

How to Sex the Leo Woman

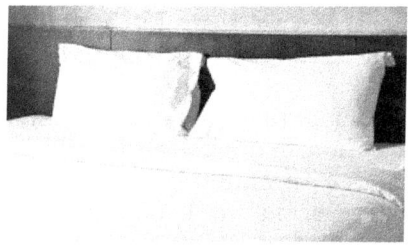

The **Leo** woman doesn't do the chasing. She sits back and waits for her prey to enter her den. She'll likely be wearing a sexy outfit she purchased from Victoria's Secret. She knows she's alluring.

Finding Your Perfect Sexual Match by Lysa London

She knows the animal magnetism she has inside. If you're her man, you'll be treated like a king. Don't push or force, allow the lioness to set the pace.

Start with your tongue on her thighs working your way up and into her opening; hands free-no fingers-all tongue. She likes to climb on top so that the man can engulf her breasts. She also likes to watch him as he's watching her; that's why she keeps the lights on.

She's not inclined to try new things in the bedroom unless you persuade her. The **Leo** woman feels like the old ways work best. If it's not broke don't fix it. Once you get her hot you'd better be up to the task or she'll make you feel less than a man without saying a single word.

Anyone who knows the **Leo** woman knows she likes to run things in the bedroom. If she's into you or if you're her man she won't mind sharing power. But **Leo** women who don't exercise restraint can fall into really dark, domineering and sadistic sex.

Although **Leo** is not one of the kinky, buck nasty signs, she does have those tendencies that can escalate and get out of control. She may put on a strap on and convince her man to bend over. She may put on high heels and walk across his back. She may also seduce teenage boys that she can control and who will do exactly what she says without question.

Finding Your Perfect Sexual Match by Lysa London

***The Leo woman is most compatible with Aries, Gemini and Sagittarius.*

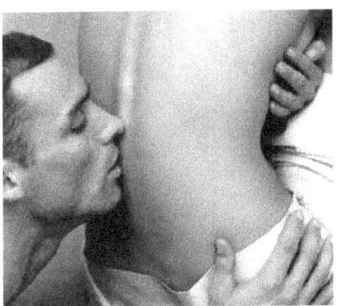

Soft touches with a feather, your moist lips, or even your fingertips turns Leo women up and on.

Finding Your Perfect Sexual Match by Lysa London

The Virgo Woman

Virgo is the Symbol of the Virgin (August 23-September 22)

If you make her angry she'll unleash a verbal hailstorm upon you the likes of which you've never heard. She's picky and not just any man will do. Her heart holds secrets and so does her mind. She has class and moves in silence; you don't want to be on her shit list.

She's an academic who will quickly research things that interest her; including people. Sometimes even over analyzing simple situations. Over thinking causes her to worry about everything. She's a stubborn type of thinker and once she sets her mind on something its next to impossible to stop her.

Finding Your Perfect Sexual Match by Lysa London

The slogan 'if you want something done right do it yourself'- had to be made up by a **Virgo** woman because she hates to lose. She demands things in her home to be a specific way; especially if she's the decorative **Virgo**. She knows her way around a kitchen so don't intrude or presume to dictate cooking policy.

She's goal oriented and expects you to be as well. But if you're not, shell put you on the right path. She is a hard taskmaster when it comes to her motherly duties; literally demanding honor roll status from her offspring. She works hard at being a good wife and will age very well. She analyzes everything; even over analyzing. So if you don't like intrusive questions, stay away from her.

When she works she expects to get paid big bucks. These days it's in technical or management positions because of her thoroughness. When it comes to her man and children **Virgo** women has vulnerability that keeps them from seeing their glaring mistakes or misconduct. She's good at getting into a man's head and knows what he's thinking before he opens his mouth. Consider it advanced stage women's intuition.

If you want to catch a Virgo woman you must be cool and collected. They like sharp, witty men. Take it easy on the sarcasm but make them laugh a bit. You can talk about something crazy that you saw on the news. But if you're a dummy, you get no respect from **Virgo**. They like their men smart-even nerdy but sexy.

How to Sex the Virgo Woman

Virgo women take sex seriously; that's why they rarely if ever casually date. She'd prefer to be in a relationship and know that you're serious about her before giving up the goodies. If she asks you over, believe me she's interested.

You just don't get lucky with **Virgo**. She actually plans to have sex with you. She's not dressing up to have sex. There's no sexy lingerie. It's birthday suit all the way. She's loving and tender. She will satisfy you orally and shell like doing it. She aims to please. That's right, tell her how you like it and she'll cater to you. Making you happy makes her happy.

Virgo women view sex as part of their womanly duties to their men. However, there's a secret she doesn't tell her man; she likes being spanked with a wide belt. The idea and feeling of punishment makes her boiling hot. She's guaranteed to pull down her panties after that!

*The Virgo Woman is most compatible with Cancer, Taurus, and Scorpio.

Spank that ass and watch her become unhinged!

Finding Your Perfect Sexual Match by Lysa London

The Libra Woman

Libra is the Symbol of the Scales
(September 23-October 22)

Men, you're going to find out **Libra** women are very attractive. Men rave about how hot their butts look in jeans. They dress sexy with a fragrance nothing short of enticing. **Libra** women have an eye for nice things. She looks for styles and trends that are hot.

She prefers attractive men that stand out. She wants you to be in good shape with a tone body. She is very enticing and equally as stubborn. Be nice to her when she's upset and you just might get your way.

She is guided by Venus the Goddess of love and lust. The **Libra** woman can be wishy- washy when it comes to male suitors; throwing one aside for another. But her ideal man is in the entertainment business; not the nine to fiver. She's enticed by the bright lights and big city atmosphere.

The **Libra** and Leo women share the same need to be seen; they like to shine. And their charisma and attitude is truly contagious; often brightening your party or event. She hates cheap men and can be a bitch when things don't go her way. She likes things done right the first time; borderline perfectionist with many layers.

If you take her out, shower her with compliments about the things most guys wouldn't notice. But keep it real. As far as conversation goes, she'll be pretty liberal. On special occasion give her something odd, shiny and blingy. Take her to a classy restaurant then go see a chic flick; romantic comedy.

Libra women love their body and like to show off their curves. They often go without brazier or panties and want you to notice.

How to Sex the Libra Woman

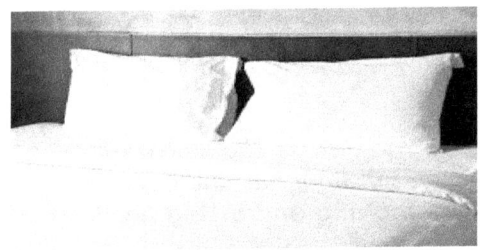

She likes to dress up sexy for her man and often use costly perfume (take notice!). She wants you to take your time. Soft, love-making music will help. Go ahead and massage her body with warm oil. That will make her incredibly wet.

Be Warned: **Libra** women have that snapper- as the old school men use to call it. In other words, she can control her vagina muscles. A lot of men say that she can clamp down on their penis' and cause them to moan with sheer delight.

She doesn't like it rough, though; so don't even try it. No pulling, tugging or choking; sorry. She's a girly girl- in and out of the bedroom. And by all means, please, don't forget to tell her how good it was.

Libra Women are most compatible with Leo, Aquarius and Gemini.

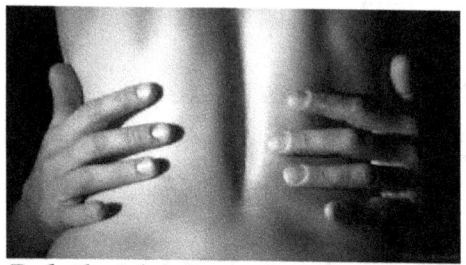

Rub that booty and caress the small of her back and watch how hot she gets. That includes pinching and biting her buttocks.

Finding Your Perfect Sexual Match by Lysa London

The Scorpio Woman

Scorpio is the Symbol of the Scorpion
(October 23-November 21)

Men, Scorpio women know how to get a man's attention. She knows how to keep his attention too. She can open a man's nose quick; almost as if he was hypnotized. She can force an impotent man to stand at attention if you know what I mean. Don't be tight, cheap or stingy; she hates a tight wad. You're going to be digging into your pocket if you want her.

It takes a real man's man to catch a Scorpio woman. **Scorpio** women like to go... go... go. They have a lot of energy. She's deeply loyal to the man she loves and will bend over backwards for him. She will also put anyone in check who talks shit about him. She has the ability to see through your secrets while

Finding Your Perfect Sexual Match by Lysa London

keeping hers safe. Calling her stubborn would be an understatement.

Screw her over and she's like Captain Ahab chasing his whale; recklessly blind. She can become relentless and immoral when it comes to payback.

She's one of the most jealous of the zodiac signs. If you're her man, don't get caught grinning in another woman's face. She's territorial to the point of violence. **Scorpio** women will swear to god that you're cheating if you ever get caught in a lie.

She loves the alpha male and thinks nothing of weak or timid men. Arguing with her is like contending with hell on wheels. She will cuss you six ways from Sunday when she's mad. She is even more volatile then the Aries female. If you're an alpha male in search of a ride or die chick, **Scorpio** woman will seriously have your back.

If you're hunting a **Scorpio** woman try a candle light dinner at your place. Put on soft music and nice cologne. But if you decide to eat out try the Red Lobster buffet. She loves fresh seafood.

All women love compliments, but **Scorpio** women more- so then most. Stay on script and don't be disagreeable. Turn off your cell phone and no texting. She demands your undivided attention; anything less will be an argument and you'll eventually turn her off. Hold hands and keep close contact. She likes affection. And when the sparks start to fly make sure you bought you're A-game.

How to Sex the Scorpio Woman

Get ready because arguably one of the freakiest signs of the zodiac will give you a night you won't forget. A Scorpio woman probably coined the phrase **"be a lady in the streets and a freak in the sheets."**

If a Scorpio woman wants you, she's coming after you. She will control, direct and command the bedroom. Scorpio woman will wear sexy clothes and costumes. She'll use sexual devices on herself and she'll use them on you, too.

She wants a big, comfortable bed. She wants you to get yours, but she demands that she gets hers too; multiple times. She's not taking her ipad to bed if she notices a stiff erection that needs tending. Ideally, she'll do both.

She also has dominatrix tendencies. Her need to dominate and sometimes object penetrate her partners are well known. This often leads Scorpio women to lesbianism if her man isn't passive enough in the bedroom. So, if you want to keep her- do what you're told.

*The Scorpio female is most compatible with Pisces, Capricorn and Cancer.

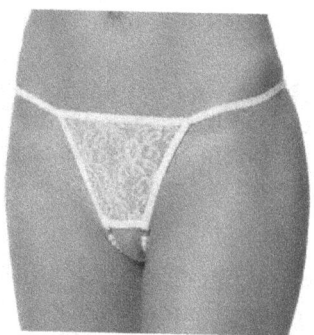

Scorpio woman's hot spot is anything dealing with her clit.

Finding Your Perfect Sexual Match by Lysa London

The Sagittarius Woman

Sagittarius is the Symbol of the Archer

(November 22-December21))

Men, first things first; the **Sagittarius** woman loves herself, her beauty, her booty and her voice. She has no problem saying what's on her mind. Overall, she's a big hearted and kind woman. She always needs to be doing something. She's energetic and likes to come and go as she pleases.

She has no problem with casual sex; mostly for the excitement. She hates being bored-in love and life. She's funny, optimistic and gets along with the opposite sex just fine. If she's your woman, a man will never claim his woman doesn't listen; she's good at that.

Finding Your Perfect Sexual Match by Lysa London

If you like football, basketball, rock climbing or bungee jumping, she's your girl. Her charismatic nature can bring people together effortlessly; parties, cook-outs, and other social gatherings.

Sagittarius women are flirty and sometimes she acts like she knows everything; you know the type. It's a trait that keeps her stubborn. Impulsiveness clouds her view and she finds herself in situations that could have been avoided by asking the right questions early on.

Although a consummate flirt and free flowing with some men, the one who takes her heart will wound her deeply if he leaves. Her sensitive nature can't handle insults or pranks.

Sweet talk works better and sometimes too well. Scandalous men latch on and are hard for her to break free of. **Sagittarius** women can sometimes come off as airheads but even with her faults you can't hold them down.

To catch a **Sagittarius** woman you must be sharp with spontaneous banter or else approach another sign because she's not listening. Spark up a conversation about pets and take her to an outdoor sporting event; NASCAR, hockey or a carnival. She loves the outdoors and the unusual; try for both.

How to Sex the Sagittarius Woman

Men, if there's something about you that she likes, guess what; you're going to get laid. Her approach to numerous sexual partners is cavalier. And if the relationship is going bad, don't be upset if she's the one who says **"maybe we should just be friends."**

Sex on the beach was named after her- because it's her favorite place to have sex. She also likes to do it in the park-after dark. She likes it on a bench, a wooded area, on a mountain top, on the hood of a car; anywhere outside. And she likes to get down to business; so skip the appetizers and bring on the main course. Remember; touching, feeling and rubbing aren't always necessary.

She wants what she wants in bed; to hell with how you feel about it. She gives oral and she gets on top. She loves having sex and her first priority is her own orgasm; not yours. She doesn't mind leaving you with heavy nuts.

Sometimes if you experience premature ejaculation be prepared for her to climb right back on. And if you don't get hard soon, she'll talk cold, hard trash to you and insult your manhood. You better make sure she's satisfied. She doesn't necessarily cuddle but she does enjoy the pillow talks. If you act "pussy whipped" afterwards, she's not going to respect you.

To the **Sagittarius** woman, love and sex are not interchangeable and she can at times appear detached from both. Certain men, with traits that she's attracted to (for example: a heavy beard, bald head, tattoos etc.) can often end up in her bed. If you catch her cheating and she says ***"it meant nothing to me,"*** believe me, it meant nothing.

The ninth sign of the zodiac is not into toys or gadgets. She's not a super-freak, so don't look for foot fetishes, food fetishes, whips, chains, blindfolds or handcuffs; just good old fashioned sex. But her strong throat and vaginal muscles are enough to impress and climax any man.

The **Sagittarius** woman's wayward attitude towards sex can also lead to threesomes and other women. In a lesbian relationship, she'll assume the masculine role.

*Sagittarius women are most compatible with Leo, Aquarius, Libra and sometimes Aries.

Finding Your Perfect Sexual Match by Lysa London

An oily massage of her butt and thighs will get you what you want every time.

Finding Your Perfect Sexual Match by Lysa London

The Capricorn Woman

Capricorn is the Symbol of the Goat (December 22-January 19)

Men, this highly organized woman isn't the tight-ass you may think she is. She just likes things to go smoothly. She'd love to give herself to you completely but she hesitates out of an underlying fear.

She is a well disciplined sign. No matter how horny she gets, her panties will not simply slide off for you. She's leery about relationships because she looks for the long term commitment. To most men, she's the one who got away.

Finding Your Perfect Sexual Match by Lysa London

She is an unusually loyal sign and will go all in on a relationship. Once a Capricorn woman establishes that you're hers, she'll do anything for you. But don't cross her because she'll hold that grudge forever. She likes being sexy-classy; make-up, nails, hair-the whole nine yards.

The young Capricorn woman is quiet and subdued. But as the years go by she'll become more focused and sure. She's goal oriented and doesn't play games when it comes to her money or agenda. She's always busy doing something constructive.

She may seem kind of cold. But that's just a defense mechanism. It may appear at times she's acting stuck up but it's just her keeping her guard up until she gets to know you. Say something nice to melt the ice. Don't give cornball compliments. She hates phony pick up lines. Capricorn women are resilient. It may take her a while to get where she's going but she gets there despite what hurdles she must overcome.

To catch the eye of the Capricorn woman you must be doing some volunteer work or helping some poor kids. She likes thinkers and doers; not hacks or posers. She's sentimental about family and collectables. They like nice food in good surroundings.

Make sure that your house is clean and nicely decorated. Don't invite her over if your place is run down and dirty. You need to show style and class.

She has been known to change Mr. Wrong into her Mr. Right. But you must at least be moldable.

How to Sex the Capricorn Woman

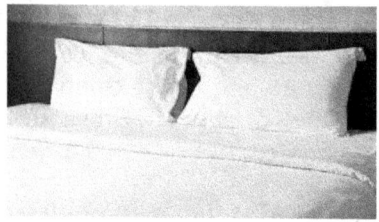

You can't be one of those guys with a premature ejaculate. She likes multiple orgasms and expects you to deliver. She likes it when you go down on her. And she'll do you back to make sure you're nice and hard- just for her. Press your thumb against her clitoris. When she's hot all she thinks about is her orgasm. She's like a fiend and your penis is her drug.

Don't waste your time with a bunch of wild positions, they'll serve only your ego; she's cool with the basics. She likes to get on top. She likes to make noise, bite and scratch. She wants you to give her multiple orgasms. And expects to have sex regularly; on her schedule- not yours.

Now, don't be surprised if your **Capricorn** woman asks you to take a dildo to the rear. Yes, I'm talking about her pushing some kind of device up your anus. She may want to tie you up and beat you with a cat- o- nine tails. Dishing out pain gives her sexual pleasure and heightens her passions. Be warned...and ready!

*Capricorn Women are most compatible with Scorpio, Taurus, Pisces and sometimes Capricorn

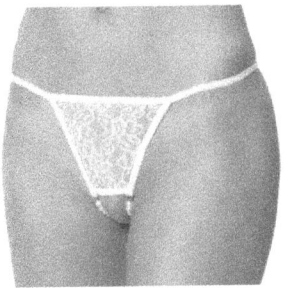

Thumb on the clitoris and under her armpit. Those are her secret hot spots.

Finding Your Perfect Sexual Match by Lysa London

Follow: twitter @ LysaLondon
Email: Lysalondon@gmail.com